# UNDERNEATH THE LINTEL

An Impressive Presentation of
Lovely Evidences

The alternate version:
in which the Librarian
is a woman

*Glen Berger*

**BROADWAY PLAY PUBLISHING INC**
56 E 81st St., NY NY 10028-0202
212 772-8334  fax: 212 772-8358
BroadwayPlayPubl.com

UNDERNEATH THE LINTEL (female version)
© Copyright 2007 by Glen Berger

All rights reserved. This work is fully protected
under the copyright laws of the United States of
America.
No part of this publication may be photocopied,
reproduced, stored in a retrieval system,
or transmitted, in any form or by any means,
electronic, mechanical, recording, or otherwise,
without the prior permission of the publisher.
Additional copies of this play are available from
the publisher.
Written permission is required for live
performance of any sort. This includes readings,
cuttings, scenes, and excerpts. For amateur and
stock performances, please contact Broadway Play
Publishing Inc. For all other rights contact Joyce
Ketay, The Gersh Agency, 41 Madison Ave, 33rd
fl, NY NY 10010.

First printing: August 2007
I S B N: 0-88145-287-4

Book design: Marie Donovan
Word processing: Microsoft Word
Typographic controls: Xerox Ventura Publisher 2.0
P E
Typeface: Palatino
Printed and bound in the U S A

# ABOUT THE AUTHOR

Glen Berger is a sixth-year member of New Dramatists. His plays include: UNDERNEATH THE LINTEL (Over 450 performances Off-Broadway, Ovation Award (Los Angeles), Sterling Award (Edmonton), and Connecticut Critics Circle Award for Best Play, Garland Award for Best Playwriting, and one of *Time Out* New York's Ten Best Plays of 2001, productions in over sixty cities in eight countries), THE WOODEN BREEKS (nominated for Best Writing by the *L A Weekly*, 2001), O LOVELY GLOWWORM (2005 Portland Drammy Award Winner for Best Script), the musical A NIGHT IN THE OLD MARKETPLACE, (Loewe Award), GREAT MEN OF SCIENCE, NOS. 21 & 22 (1998 Ovation Award and 1998 L.A. Weekly Award for Best Play), I WILL GO...I WILL GO (published in Applause Book's 2001 *Best Short Plays* Anthology), and the musical ON WORDS AND ONWARDS (Manhattan Theater Club/Sloan Foundation Fellowship). Glen has received commissions from the Children's Theater of Minneapolis, Berkeley Rep, the Alley Theater, and the Lookingglass Theater. He has received six Emmy nominations, writing episodes for children's television series including *Arthur*

(P B S), its spin-off *Postcards From Buster*, *Time Warp Trio* (N B C), *Peep* (Discovery Channnel), and *Fetch* (P B S), for which he's the head writer.

The first official production of the female version of UNDERNEATH THE LINTEL was at the Lederman Theater, Stockholm.

UNDERNEATH THE LINTEL was first presented at the Yale Summer Cabaret, in New Haven, for three nights in August 1999, with the author playing THE LIBRARIAN.

UNDERNEATH THE LINTEL was produced by The Actors' Gang, Patti McGuire, producer, in Los Angeles for a limited run in May 2001. The cast and creative contributors were:

THE LIBRARIAN ......................Brian T Finney

*Director & designer* ...............Brent Hinkley
*Stage manager* ...................Byrne Lethnik

UNDERNEATH THE LINTEL premiered Off-Broadway at the Soho Playhouse, opening on October 23, 2001, and produced by Scott Morfee, Tom Wirtshafter, and Dana Matthow. The cast and creative contributors were:

THE LIBRARIAN ......................T Ryder Smith

*Director* ......................... Randy White
*Set design* ..................... Lauren Helpern
*Projection design consultant* ..... Elaine McCarthy
*Lighting design* .................. Tyler Micoleau
*Sound design* .................... Paul Adams
*Costume* ................... Miranda Hoffman
*Production stage manager* .........Richard Hodge
*Production coordinator* .............Cris Buchner

In January 2002, David Chandler took over the role of THE LIBRARIAN.

# SETTING & CHARACTER

*Setting: Here*

*Time: Now*

*The* LIBRARIAN *has rented the space for the night,
and didn't have much to spend on it. Perhaps the
auditorium we're in is has been "dark" for some time,
or perhaps the theatre is "between shows." Props and
other detritus from other shows can litter the back of the
stage, or be seen in an exposed back room. An air of
dilapidation would be fine. Perhaps the* LIBRARIAN
*is giving this lecture in a seedier part of town,
on a rainy night, to four or five down-and-outs
more interested in getting in from the rain than
listening to a lecture by a woman from the Netherlands.
Over the course of the evening however, the "lecture"
should imperceptibly turn into "theater." The detritus,
unnoticed and seemingly unimportant at first, can
unexpectedly take on significance, alluding to scenes
and history mentioned in the play. The lighting can
become warmer, more "theatrical", etc., and what
seemed like a random strewing of objects, or a random
water stain on the wall, for instance, can turn out to
be not so random after all.*

*Character: Dutch because: The Dutch have a
wonderfully bureaucratic streak in them (or so
I'm told). They also tend to have a facility for other*

*European languages, and I've known more than one person from the Netherlands who had remarkable English, with a nearly imperceptible accent. Point is, the accent should be very light, and the actor should pay more attention to developing the "idiolect", meaning "an individual's unique way of speaking."*

*Like the set, the character should imperceptibly transform over the evening. Perhaps she removes the jacket she's wearing as the performance proceeds; sleeves get rolled up; hair gets loose from the pins keeping it in place, etc.*

*One last note: THE LIBRARIAN's narrative is written, generally, in the past tense. However, the less the narrative is actually presented in the past tense, the better. Immediacy, I think, is key to giving this play some theatrical life. As THE LIBRARIAN narrates how she found a claim ticket in the Baedeker's, for instance, she can "find" the claim ticket all over again.*

*Without sacrificing pacing, of course, the goal is to make THE LIBRARIAN's saga, in the end, nothing like a lecture, but rather, something that is happening now.*

*(Stage contains a chair [which should never be used for sitting], a large chalkboard [to be used at director's discretion]. There is also a battered screen for showing slides, the slide projector to be operated by the actor. An older and disheveled woman in an outfit that has seen better days appears carrying a battered suitcase full of scraps. The suitcase, once open, may have various homemade contrivances to display the "evidences.")*

*(Perhaps she also keeps certain evidences in the pockets of her dress, blouse, jacket, etc., with evidence tags dangling out.)*

*(She wears a date stamper tied with string around her neck.)*

LIBRARIAN: So. Right. We'll proceed. I have only one night for this. I would like to have more, oh yes, but due to the extortionary rates demanded by the proprietors of this auditorium...I have only one night for this. Still. We'll proceed.

*(She points significantly to suitcase she has set down)*

Box of scraps. *Significant* scraps. Or rather... they're all I have...to *prove a life*... To prove one life...and justify another...and if you're thinking "that's a tall order for a box of scraps," well just you wait. *(With ominous significance)* They're not just scraps. *(Announcing) An Impressive Presentation of Lovely Evidences.* Hold on to your hats, gentlemen, bonnets, ladies. *(Suddenly realizing)* Hold on... *(Scanning seats)* ...is this all there is? *(Despair and indignation)* I don't know what more I can do! I put up signs, I did, on the poles, "Impressive Presentation!" but as soon as I turn my back, they're plastered over! With other signs! And mine were nicer. And important. And tomorrow, I'll be gone... *(Pondering it on a more personal level—)* ...in no time at all...I'll be gone... *(But pulls herself out of it)* ...Still. We'll proceed.

   I am...a librarian. From Hoofddorp, that's Holland. Or rather, I was, before I was fired. Or rather, I retired. Against my will. Without my pension. Or rather, that's none of your business. Or rather, it will be, but not yet. My special duty for more than many years being to check in the books that came in overnight through the overnight slot. In the back of every book, you see, there's a little envelope, and in this little envelope, there's a little card, and on that little card...*the little date the book is due. (Holds up stamper)* This is my stamper. Oh yes, I wasn't letting them keep this. It's lovely— It contains every date there ever was. You don't believe me? *(Closes eyes, fiddles with stamper dials)* "August 27, 1883," ...there, that's the date Mount Perboewaten explodes in Krakatoa, thirty-six thousand people perish under the ash. It's all in here! All the trials and joys of history. *(Closes eyes, fiddles with dials)* "January 25, 1971"...oh, January 25, 1971...Helen...Shattock is walking her dog in Dayton, Ohio when a frozen block of urine from the lavatory of a Pan Am jet, falls, and hits her on the head, killing her instantly. Mind you, *(Fiddles with stamper)* same date, "1836",

Cetewayo, King of the Zulus is born! oh yes,
this stamper contains every birth in this room,
not just Cetewayo's. And death. Yes, our deaths
too...somewhere... My death is in here...
somewhere...I just don't know...where... Still.
Gives you a bit of respect for it, doesn't it.
The stamper.

So. Yes. So, each and every day I woke up, took
the bus, no, no husband, no children, I lived alone,
got to the bibliotheque, put my labeled lunch in
the employees icebox, gave a but-just-perceptible
nod to Floris van der Donk, works in reference
lovely lady I'm sure except that I'm sure that
she's not and always angling for that acquisitions
position that by all rights is mine, I'm the next
in line!, em, arrived at my desk, yes that's next,
quieted the patrons, "ssh," and advanced the
date on my little stamper...one notch.

Now listen, the overnight slot is strictly for those
books *not overdue*. But we checked anyway. That
was my job. To check. Now and then you'd find
a book a day or two overdue. Sometimes a week.
Once, a book was returned, in the slot mind you,
three months overdue—well we got over it, but
we weren't amused. And neither was the violator
when he saw the fine ho ho. Still. We'll proceed.
One morning— *(She writes "1986" on the chalkboard)*
One fine and miserable and typical morning,
nothing to give an inkling of what was to come—
*(Significantly)* I found this book in the pile.

*(She takes out a battered book from the box with a tag
attached to it labeled "Evidence #1")*

LIBRARIAN: We'll label it Eveydence #1. It is a
Baedeker's travel guide, in deplorable condition.
Well, I was just about to give the little card my
stamp with the old stamper when my eyes
suddenly sprang out of my head and rolled
about on the floor and under the table. And why?
Because I saw that this book was checked out
in 1873 and no...no—never returned til it was
returned. Do you understand? *(She writes "1873"
on the chalkboard, and demonstrates the math.)*
That's a one-hundred-and-thirteen years...
overdue! Astounded out of my wits I was.
It must have been the great great grandson
returning the book, a blot on the family only
now being remedied. And returned in the
overnight slot no less! Appalling. If you have
a book one hundred and thirteen years
overdue...you go to the counter, you admit your
lapse, you pay the fine. Well, whoever it was,
he wasn't getting away with it, not a chance,
I checked the files—oh yes, we keep all the files,
and I found the page and here it is. *(She takes out a
page from a ledger labeled:)* "Eveydence #2." *(Reads)*
"Baedeker's Travel Guide, checked out November
12th, 1873 by capital A...period." *(Writes "A." on
chalkboard)* That's the name. Capital A. Period.
About as vague as they come, but never mind,
what's his address, so I can send him the fine of
his life. *(Reads)* "Post Office Box 121, Dingtao."
Well Dingtao didn't ring any bells so I got out the
old Atlas. *(She procures an atlas and pages through it.)*
I've always liked atlases. They allow you to travel
all over the world—*without the expense.* Yes it's
true, I had never left Holland. I had rarely left

Hoofddorp. I went to Gouda once to see how they
made the cheese. But the tour wasn't given that
day, I don't know why, so never mind. Here it is,
Dingtao, near Kaifeng. And no, it seems Kaifeng
is not near Hoofdorp. No. Nor Rotterdam. No.
It's China! Now how a Chinaman managed to
check out a book from a Dutch library without
a residence in the Netherlands, well—that would
be the first of many puzzlers in this twisty mystery
of a tale. And was he even a Chinaman? After all,
the notes scrawled in the margins of the book were
written in every language under the sun. Including
Welsh. Well, it was none of my business. I filled
out the standard form notifying our man of the
pretty fine awaiting him, and bunged it off to
China, and that was that.

But was that really that? No. That was not in any
way...that. I couldn't get the miscreant out of my
mind. I didn't reshelve the book, no, I thumbed
through it. I took it home with me. I carried it
about. And one day as I was flipping through it,
I came upon this. *(Pulls from book)* Eveydence #3.
Bookmark. But not just any bookmark. No.
A bookmark by proxy. An unredeemed claim
ticket for one pair of trousers left in a Chinese
Laundering establishment. Oh, in China? No.
In London. In *(Writes on chalkboard)* 1913,
seventy-three years previous. Well. My life went
on, the bus, the books, the "how are you today,
Floris," and "no, I don't believe my lunch is taking
up too much room in the ice box, Floris, no, well,
I'm sorry you feel that way," and the organizing
of the cart and a "have a good night yourself" and
then off with the lights and home again, but I'll say

this...I got to thinking about those trousers. In fact, I couldn't *stop* thinking about those trousers. In fact I had more than one *dream* about those trousers, Trousers, Trousers, Trousers, Trousers until I couldn't take it anymore. Never claimed! Oh sure, the shop probably went defunct years ago, but perhaps...*not*. But of course, what was I going to do—fritter away my vacation days just to go to London for some non-existent trousers? Hah. I don't think so. No. On the contrary. *(Beat)* I *applied* to travel to London on *library business*. *(Eagerly)* To claim the trousers you see on behalf of the library to recoup some of the losses the library would no doubt accrue from the unpaid fine. It was, perhaps, the most daring gambit I had ever devised, but I felt I was on solid ground, and what do you know, the application was...rejected. Flat out. With a reprimand attached about "frivolous requests". Oh I was beside myself and I did a bit of inconspicuous sulking, and then a bit of conspicuous sulking, and then I was calm again. But damn it to hell, I still couldn't get the pants out of my head, so I went to London all the same....

*(We hear the '30s tune,* Life Begins at Oxford Circus, *or similarly jaunty 30s-vintage tune from an English "sweet" band)*

LIBRARIAN: ...expending...precious...vacation...time.

*(And we see slides of London as—)*

LIBRARIAN: London. Dear God the Chaos! The bustle! Oh this was a terrible mistake, why wasn't I home in Hoofddorp in front of the goggle box, cup of tea, nothing ever on but I didn't mind,

tall red buses and sweet shops run by Pakistanis—
and not very good sweets at that—and the Bloody
Tower and the Roman Wall and to think this all
used to be swamps and mastodons. "What's this?
Something for the French tourist—*Les Miserables*—
that looks interesting—"the miserable"—It's all
about me in London," I thought, and I had never
seen a play before, so I paid, and it's true, after two
hours, I was more "miserables" than I had ever
been before. Still, we'll proceed.

To the Holloway Road and the Chinese Laundry
and...well what do you know, it was still there.
The shop. So I strode in, waved around my claim
ticket, and I came out with a pair of trousers. *(From
the box she extrudes—)* Eveydence #4. Trousers. And
never cleaned in all that time because they were in
such a state of disrepair to begin with. A common
laundering policy apparently, to protect the shop
from accusations of negligence, but I was the
gladder for it, because it meant that any clues
would be left *in situ*, as they say.

And I was rewarded. I checked the pockets and
I found...this. *(She extrudes from pocket with evidence
tag attached—)* A used tram ticket. Eveydence #5.
From *1912*. A tram that ran in Bonn. Ger-ma-ny.

*(And we hear the tune* Ungarwein *by von Geezy
and his Orchestra, or similarly vaguely Germanic
thirties-vintage upbeat and librarian-inspiring tune
[a song by the Comedian Harmonists, e.g.] and see
a slide of Bonn and the Municipal Transportation
Headquarters)*

LIBRARIAN: Well I don't know what got into me,
feverish, I took a bus to Bonn, to the Municipal

Transportation Headquarters to read up on
Incident reports for the month of March 1912.
Oh yes, I was a regular detective now. It was a
shot in the dark, I know, but I figured any scofflaw
making loose with the library rules might have
made some trouble on a tram in Bonn as well.
Well you never know. And hey ho, look at what
I found. *(She takes out from his box—)* A photeystat
I'll label #6, and reads, in the German, as written
by the tram conductor, as follows— *"Ein Mann
mit einem Bart und einem neu— (Stops short, to
audience—) Sprechen sie—*oh, no, perhaps not...em,
let's see... *(And she translates—)* "A man with beard
and curious hat and smelling truly foul, boarded
the tram at Potsdamer Platz with a mangy dog.
Although there were plenty of seats, he *refused
to sit,* and instead paced up and down the aisle
with his dog distracting the other passengers
and myself. A dirty Jew, I threw him off at
Wittlesbach."

Well, surely this wasn't the same man as the man
who owned these trousers, but there was a chance,
slim, and I was hooked. And I hated it! What was
I doing in Bonn!?—there's always something about
German food that gives me— *(She's said too much
and now it's too late)* ...well it gives me flatus...
*(More awkwardness)* ...wind... *(Unjustifiably peevish
toward audience)* ...and why that's any concern of
yours I have no idea... *(Quickly turning to Baedeker's
to change subject)* Bonn, devastated by the
Normans, rebuilt, devastated by Frederick III,
rebuilt, devastated yet again in World War Two...
rebuilt! In a chocolate shop I knocked over an
enormous display of marzipan and by the end

of the day, it was...rebuilt. Moved to tears by the
humanity of it all. The persistence, the forbearance.
Or I would have been, if "A Period" hadn't kept
doing the backstroke across my brain, who is he!
No no, I needed a distraction. Quick—I ducked
into a playhouse, showing a play called *(Perplexed
and dismayed)* ...*Les Miserables*. It was exactly the
same. Only worse. And it was no distraction!—The
tram, the trousers, the travel guide, I had to find
out more about this man, But how? A dead end it
seemed. "Curious hat" "smelling foul" "threw him
off at Wittlesbach" Hang on. What's that about a
dog. *(Draws a dog on the chalkboard)* He had a dog, it
said, in Germany, in 1912. And he was in England
in *1913* long enough to drop off his trousers. But!
For the past one hundred years there's been a law
in England—all dogs from foreign countries must
be put in quarantine *(Draws prison cell around dog)*
for six months on the grounds of Rabies
Prevention, there being no rabies in England.
Could it be then that our man was forced to
leave his dog in English quarantine? Because, if so,
there would be records! I called in to Hoofddorp
extending my vacation, ignored the grumblings on
the other end, worried a little about giving Floris
the one-up but I'd attend to that, and like a shot,
I was back on British soil, rifling through files
for dogs deposited between March 1912 and
November 1913, and here was something very
curious— Only one dog, stay with me here, one
dog alone, was put in quarantine during that
period, who, after six months, was not reclaimed.
That dog's name was... *(Writes on chalkboard)*
...Sabrina....

*(We hear a scratchy recording of* It's a Long Way to Tipperary *[preferably by John McCormack or similar W W I-vintage war song] and see a slide of soldiers in trenches.)*

LIBRARIAN: Sabrina. October 1914 and Sabrina still not claimed. World War I had started by then, ten million men would be slaughtered by the end, and the German dog, Sabrina, she too was put down, at last... Gassed... And as I stood there in that office, I began to wonder... *(Looks about)* What was I doing here?! But! And yet! What was that dog doing here. And what was anybody doing in those trenches in 1914— *(To slide of soldier)* oh but you doughboys had a song for that, didn't you, how did it go— *(Sings waveringly but jauntily the old soldier song. [To tune of* Auld Lang Syne*])* "We're here because we're here because we're here because we're here...." Yes, well enough of that. The veterinarian's report on Sabrina is a tearjerker and reads in part— (Reading scrap of paper with Evidence label dangling on it) "This dog was brought to us with its footpads torn to shreds. And yet, when we told the dog to sit, it whined and whimpered, and refused to sit, and cowered in terror, as if sitting would bring with it a terrible beating." Poor Sabrina! And remember now, our man in the tram was reported as pacing up and down, *refusing to sit.* Well. This was getting interesting. *(Apologizing to audience)* Not riveting. But interesting. And nothing else of note except this, Except this!— *(Reveals, attached to the report, with its own evidence tag)* a release statement, handwritten by our Mister Mystery, oh yes, matching to a tee all the loops of the ells and

ees that we have here in the margins of the bloody
Baedekers! And he signed it— *"A" period*. And he
wrote, "I give full authorization to these fellows to
keep for the proscribed allotment of time, my dog,
*Zebrina*." Not Sabrina. But "Ze." With a Z, E
Zebrina. Well. "What sort of a name is that?"
I wondered. So I looked it up in the dictionary,
and encyclopedia, and one of those "name-the-
baby" books and do you know what I found?
Nothing. Still. I tucked it away in the back of the
thinking thing that I cleverly carry around with
me, sometimes, and there was this too—our man
was required on this form to leave the name and
address of a man in the Country who could vouch
for him, and he wrote "the estate of the Lord of
Derby, Attention: Thomas Wright."

And here's where things take a turn. And I'm
talking about my stomach, for one. And here's
why. I did a bit of research. Thomas Wright did
live on the estate of the Lord of Derby, oh yes...
but it was **almost two hundred years previous
to the date of the Release Statement, Thomas
Wright lived on the estate of the Lord of Derby
from 1720 to 1754.** *1754*. Two-hundred-and-
thirty-two years before the Baedeker's Book
was returned. Well this didn't make any sense.
I was a bit scared now...no one lives that long....
Surely...surely he wrote down the first name that
came to his head, having no one truly who could
vouch for him in England... Surely! But if you
think I wasn't up in Derby the next day, to the
archives now overseen by the National Trust,
sifting through the account books of Thomas
Wright, well, you'd be wrong. This was getting

funny, and I didn't like it.

Eveydence #9. A page from Wright's Account Book. Whose now? Thomas Wright's. He kept the accounts of the estate of the Lord of Derby. How many chamberpots ordered and whatnot. And a diligent man was he. And good for us. And here's why. Year, 1748. Page 112, line 8— "Earthstopper— hired for week. Four pence." So what? So this—in the margins next to the line, and on the back of the page, Wright scribbled the following — *(And she acts out the following in a clearly rehearsed, but rather stiltedly rendered, performance [though still managing to impart an air of mystery to "the man in the funnel-shaped hat"]—)*

> Whilst riding in coach, early evening, encountered a most curious man wearing faded yellow funnel-shaped hat roaming grounds of estate.
>
> "Sir," I said, "You are trespassing on private ground belonging to the Lord of Derby, you don't belong here."
>
> "I *don't* belong here, I don't belong anywhere at all, but I'm everywhere nonetheless and you can thank your Lord for that."
>
> "Do you have a grievance with my Lord?"
>
> "You don't know the half of it", he replied, in an accent impossible to place, but if I had to venture, I would say half-French, half...monkey.
>
> "May I ask how my Lord has grieved you, sir?"
>
> "You may ask, but I mayn't answer—I'm not allowed to tell you how he has wronged me."
>
> "Then how do you expect my Lord of Derby to make amends", I said, rather exasperated. And here, the curious man doubled over, and said

that was the funniest joke he had ever heard.
He said evidently we have been talking about
two different Lords. Well, obviously an escapee
from Bedlam, but suddenly remembering that
I was in desperate need of an earthstopper for
tomorrow's hunt, I took the liberty of asking
this crooked man if he would like a night's
employment. At the word "earthstopper",
his eyes lit up.

Hold on. Stop the narrative. What's earthstopping.
Well, let's look it up.

*(We see a slide of Joseph Wright's 19th century painting*
The Earthstopper)

LIBRARIAN: Oh yes, here's a picture of it and a
faded miserable picture it is. Apparently it's a little
tactic developed by the foxhunting gentry. Foxes,
apparently, live in dens, snug little places.... At
night, the foxes leave their dens, and skulk about,
looking for supper. Otherwise, it's the dens for
them. Well, if you live on a big estate, and you're
throwing a foxhunting party in the morning,
you don't want all the foxes in their dens, no.
Your guests will say, one and all, "well that was
a lousy party." So what do you do. You employ
an *earthstopper*, who goes out with his lantern and
spade the night before, and while the fox is out,
he stops up his den right up to the top with earth.
When the fox returns, he can't find his home,
"what miserable earthstopper's done this," says
the fox, "burying my wife and all my lovelies,
and now I must roam the hills til morn and find
a fix to this conundrum" And, of course, in the
morn—while the fox is aroaming—the dogs, the

horns, the horses, the slaughter. Lovely. Now back
to the narrative.

> ...At the word "earthstopper", his eyes lit up.
> "Oh, are you one who appreciates a good
> hunt?"
> "Well no, I like the idea of the little fox roaming
> about with no place to return to—it's...funny."
> As he appeared exhausted I bade him ride in
> the coach, which he did, but he would not sit.
> When I insisted he sit, he insisted with equal
> force he would not. Unable to abide by a man
> who insists on standing stooped in front of me
> in a coach, I bade him walk on behind until...

And here the little anecdote suddenly and forever
stops, the next page missing, you see...Thomas
Wright, you see, grew liquidy in the mind, over
time, and the little children would steal in, and
steal his official papers to use for kites, and the life
of Wright got snagged in trees and down
drainpipes. *(With unexpected bitterness)* And whose
doesn't. But! We have this. A man who wouldn't
sit on a coach, a man who wouldn't sit on a tram,
a man's dog who wouldn't sit in a kennel, a man
with a grievance against some lord, and a man
with a funny hat. Well. I'm no mathematician,
but even I could see that it was beginning to
add up. *(Beat)* Not that I was bad in mathematics,
mind you. Next to Maarten Roosberg, I was top
in my class, for a year. And that's where I met him
actually. Maarten. In math. Oh he had a wonderful
brain for..what are those things...variables. We'd
do our homework after school, that's how it
started. Fine old time though—giggling, of all

things..I wasn't even supposed to be in his class but I was transferred over, heaven knows why... *(Now intensely introspective)* ...there's a thought for you... *(And comes out of it when she notices the audience)* Oh,yes, well enough of that, em, look at this.

*(We see a slide projected—)*

LIBRARIAN: This is a page from a fourteenth century German manuscript, depicting a man with a yellow funnel-shaped hat. He's of the Hebraic faith. How do I know? Because all men of the Hebraic faith had to wear a funny hat just like this one. *In the fourteenth century*, that is. All of this weighed heavily on the mind as I returned to the day-to-day in Hoofddorp. I stamped, oh yes, I filed, I fined, but *inside* the brains were churning like the machinery in a cheese factory. When it isn't closed. I had clues, eveydence, but what did it mean? The patrons were noisy, I didn't care, overdue books came in, I didn't care, someone stole my lunch from the icebox, I..cared, but not as much as I would have.

And then, one day, *it happened*. I was manning the information desk, when I received an urgent call, ring ring, from a patron inquiring about the amount of direct sunlight one should allow a Zebra Plant. Well I got out the handy reference guide to houseplants, turned to the index, looked up Zebra Plant, and what do you think I saw right below it? "Zebrina!" With a Z, E, As in the dog! "Zebrina Pendula. Page 130." Surely it meant absolutely nothing, but I flipped violently to the page all the same and there at the top, *(And she*

*reads in his houseplant book—)* "Zebrina Pendula,
Latin for the common houseplant Tradescantia"...
and then...a shiver...for in parentheses..."also
known as....the Wandering Jew..."

I swallowed hard. For in a little-used musty
little corner of my head, I remembered hearing
something once about a myth of a Wandering Jew.
Oh Great Guns! In a flash I dashed to the card
catalog, and "move out of my way, Floris,"
and "damn it, Floris, this is *more* important,"
and "oh wouldn't *you* like to know," and
"scramoosh, scramoosh, goodbye, scramoosh"...
made sure the coast was clear...went straight to the
drawer I needed, because I'm clever...*and found it.*

*(And she demonstrates a tattered library catalog card)*
"Tales of the Wandering Jew.")


LIBRARIAN: As the story goes, and it's been going
for centuries, there once was a cobbler, a Jew,
kept to himself, never married, stayed out of
trouble, living in Judea, around thirty-six anno
domini, although no one in the world knew it was
thirty-six anno domini...not knowing there was
a *dominus* in their midst to make it anno domini.
And can you blame them. Would you recognize
a miracle if you saw one? What if you think,
"Oh, I'll never see a miracle." Or what if you think,
"well at least I'm sure I haven't seen one yet."
What if...you're wrong?

It was April, hot day it was in Judea, the smells
of the Pesach meal the night before still lingering,
and he, our Jewish cobbler, at work with awl and
lace, in his little shop, on a shoe—when there was
a terrific shouting and haroo outside his window.

He went out on his front step and there on the
street, a procession of soldiers and convicted men
toting their crosses, no doubt to Golgotha. The
cobbler had seen it all before, and had little to say
about it—like I said, he minded his own affairs.
When suddenly, one of the frailest and sorriest of
the convicted lot collapsed, right there, right on the
steps, right by the door of our cobbler. The name
of the collapsed man was Yeshua, and he was a
mess. Well. "What do I do," thought the cobbler.
Underneath the lintel, he stood. The lintel. The top
of the doorframe. He stood under it. Yes? Good.
Underneath the lintel he stood. Not lentil...*lintel*.
Yes? You have to understand this or all is lost.
Underneath the lintel he stood, and tussled with
his quaking brain. "Let him lie on your step a
minute, let him catch his breath, it can do no
harm." But already the roman soldiers were
pressing this Yeshua to get up, and telling the
cobbler to cease in this aiding and abetting or he'd
have to answer for it himself *with a cross of his own!*,
and the cobbler was shot through and through
with fear, he had a great fear of the law, you see,
and a greater fear of death, and his hands were
forced besides, and he thought, "I don't know this
Yeshua, he's probably a thief, a murderer even,
although he doesn't look like a murderer, but
a troublemaker no doubt," and this was trouble
the cobbler could do without, so he says to this
Yeshua, he says to this man with the cross...
"get off my step...go on...move on...enough
tarrying...do your resting somewhere else!"
...And this Yeshua did get up, calmly, and turned
to the cobbler and said— "I will go...but you,

you will tarry til I come again."

And off he went, and there we go, and the cobbler didn't think twice about that little episode, and he lived to be an old man and knew his end was near, which was fine by him, by now he was sick of living. He got ill...wrote out his will...and then...he got well. Lived a few more years, got sick again, called everyone to his bedside...and then... fie upon it, he got well again. And then he began to notice an even curiouser phenomenon. He noticed, upon reaching the age of eighty, that instead of appearing older, he was looking, well, younger. And he suddenly got the urge to go for a walk, and he left his house and was never seen by his family again.

For fifty years he lived in this vagabond state, incognito, getting younger all the while, and then, he started to get older again, which went on for fifty years, and then, younger again, and fifty years of that, and on and on, older, younger, older, younger. And by this time there was more than a little groundswell claiming that this man Yeshua with the cross was more than he seemed to be, indeed...indeed, that he was the son of God...of all things...and that He would come again at the end of days as the long-awaited meshiach, and the cobbler hearing these rumours began to put two and two together, what was it that that Yeshua said? "I will go, but you, you will tarry til I come again," Holy Scamander, it all made sense to him now. He was going to be stuck on this lousy old earth until the Second Coming. "So there was a God after all," he thought. Well that's Good. And God had it in for *him* specifically. Not good. Bad.

Really awful. For over time, this Jew discovered
two stipulations of this unique curse which made
the thing more than unbearable. One—that he may
never rest. Physically impossible for him. That
means never sleep. Never lie down. Never sit
down. Never kneel. Could he lean? A little. But
just a little. So that's one stipulation, and not very
nice—I mean...sitting down...it's a wonderful
thing, a little rest, when you're exhausted, it isn't
asking much, and if you're not allowed to sit, you
become *beyond* exhausted, you just want to stop,
for a moment, and if you can't stop, then at least
crawl, on your knees, but if you're not allowed
to crawl, then you just want to die, and if you're
not allowed to die... It's grisly. But Number Two
Stipulation is just as worse, in a way, and it's
this—the Jew *can never identify himself.* He is never
allowed to confirm his own existence to his fellow
man. He can be nothing more than a myth,
whether he's a myth or not.
    Now then. Let's get one thing absolutely clear.
The Wandering Jew is a myth. Not the houseplant,
mind you. No—

*(We see a slide of houseplant.)*

LIBRARIAN: —this is a picture of the houseplant,
and as you can see, the tendrils are, shall we say,
wandering, from the pot, yes, and so it became
known as the Wandering Jew. And this is a picture
of it. And it's mine. A documented photeygraph
of the Wandering Jew zebrina pendula houseplant.
I do not have a documented photeygraph of the
Wandering Jew Jew. Everyone knows after all
that it's just a myth. A myth. As in God is a myth.

As in that old myth that life has any meaning or significance. A myth. But more and more I was becoming convinced that although the Wandering Jew was just a myth, I was in possession...of that myth's...*pants*.

The gnetleman on hold...waiting to hear about his Zebra Plant...was, regrettably, forgotten, completely. That is, until the next day when he sent a letter of complaint to my superiors—I, who had never received a complaint in my life! Oh it made dear Floris' month, I don't know how she found out about it. She even gave me a chocolate for consolation. *(Steeped in bitterness)* I didn't need her chocolate. *(Clarifying)* I ate it, but I didn't need it. So yes...yes...it was becoming clear that this overdue book was beginning to interfere...with my work...And yet I couldn't stop thinking about it!

Because...what if he *did* exist...I mean, a man *(Perhaps draws a man on the chalkboard)* living immortally, incognito, somewhere on this earth, well that's odd enough, but if he existed, it meant something even odder existed too...God...God...And all the irate Zebra Plant owners and reference department rivals in the world suddenly seemed...a little less important than they did before...I used to lose sleep over them... Now I lost sleep over something else... Mister A period. Oh yes, I forgot to mention another confounding coincidence—that in more than one source, the name of the Wandering Jew is *Ahasuerus*, do you see? Ahasuerus. As in "please initial the rental contract here, here and here Mister Ahasuerus." "Righteeo—A period, A period... A Period!"

Well. I got to thinking. If I were in such a
predicament, in which a superior had foisted
an unreasonable condition upon me, well there's
two ways you can go, either [A] accept your new
condition grovelingly, or [B] find a way around it.
I've always been more of the option [A] sort of
person myself, it's nothing to be ashamed of—
*but*—What if you've been practicing option [A]
for over a thousand years, and now you're
getting a little weary of it? A superior makes an
unreasonable demand—in this case—your life,
your history, your trials and suffering, can never
be authenticated, or even communicated, no, no,
after a thousand years, "option [B]" begins to look
better and better—*find a way around it*. Trousers,
claim tickets, incident reports—what if these
things weren't as incidental, as accidental,
or casual and trivial as they *seemed*. Just
hypothetically speaking, *you're* the hypothetical
Wandering Jew. Well wouldn't *you* drop little
clues, from time to time, nothing overt mind you,
nothing to catch His notice, but just little things...
like...oh, I don't know...conveniently leaving your
*pants*, for instance.... Or taking out a discrete post
office box in China. *(Slaps hand to forehead)* China!
Of course! The man has a post office box in China!
If I really wanted to settle this once and for all,
be done with this nonsense, all I had to do was
go to China. But! I mean....China...that seemed
just a little bit further away than, say...Neptune.
*(Drawing a brain on the chalkboard)* I put my brain
under some good hard scrutiny—it had been
playing fast and loose for too long and it needed
an audit. *(Speaks to drawing—)* "Brain! What in

heaven's name are you doing to me? Do you truly believe that this mysterious man is—" "No!" says the brain, "certainly not...or...oh...I don't know anymore"....

...thus spoke the brain...thus began the beginning of the end..because I felt myself more and more believing...I who had never believed anything in my life! *Accepted,* oh yes, I accepted plenty, But the act of *accepting* and the act of *believing* are two very different things. What was happening to me now, was a very different thing indeed.... A book drops into my lap one morning. Was it just an overdue book...or a *challenge*.... Would I recognize a miracle if I saw one...?

And yet No, this was mad mad Mad mad mad. Back to my desk, stamp stamp away, turn the notch one each day and forget about it. What was I going to do, spend all my money to go to China! I, who had Hunan Chicken, once, Once! ...and got the runs for a week! ...And there was this too... my superiors wouldn't look kindly at any more gallivanting any time soon. The overnight slot was still clogged with piled up books, and even though I had plenty of vacation time left, I was forced to sit if I had any desire to keep my job.

And so...I got ill. Oh yes, a cough, a sneeze, a swoon, and I was sent home. But... *(Confiding)* it was all a ruse! I wasn't sick at all, no!, but I had a week of sick leave to show for it! Oh clever librarian—had anybody ever thought of that before—*pretend* you're sick to get out of work— no, I don't think so, that's a new one in the books I bet.... Well I took the plunge... *(Now realizing the weight of what she's done)* ...now take the leap...

absurd, but no choice, it was off with you...to the
land of rice, the Great Wall, and...rice.

*(We hear some chinoiserie number of a 1920s/30s
vintage, e.g.* Limehouse Blues *[(Preferably by
Ambrose and his Orchestra] and see a slide of an
overcrowded Chinese city.)*

LIBRARIAN: China! A billion people. In Beijing
less than a day and I believed it. At least a billion.
And yet, it's funny, I think the death of even a
cricket is noticed because as far as I could tell, they
keep them all in cages for pets. Back in Hoofddorp,
a million insects are getting caught in a million
balls of lint behind a million couches every day
and dying and nobody knows. Mind you, *(Fiddles
with dials of stamper)* in 1887 in Honan, China, a
flood—like that! —drownded three million people,
three million! And no one in Hoofddorp batted an
eye at that either, so the insects behind the couches
shouldn't take it personally, that's just the way it
is. It may have been three million and one people
who drownded, by the way, but what's that one to
anyone but that one. If it isn't someone you know,
then it's all just...behind the couch. Of course, if I
snuffed it tomorrow, would anyone notice? Oh
yes, plenty. Or rather, a few. Or rather...Floris. But
in two hundred years, five hundred, ten thousand,
will anyone care that *she* perished? No. Or any
of us here? ...No. Lord Harry, we're all behind
the couch, mutely struggling with our lint...not
a cheery thought. Standing in Jaiseng Road in
Beijing surrounded by a billion other souls can
do that to your thoughts, a diversion was needed,
I tried to get tickets for a show in town called...

*Les Miserables*—yes, I like it, I admit it—but I was mistakenly given tickets to the Peking Opera instead, and I went, and...I liked that too...I didn't know what was happening to me.... I had heard that travel broadened the mind but at this rate I would need a sombrero soon. But on to Dingtao, where I greased a palm, a very easy thing to do in Dingtao, as if our man had foreseen it all, and I obtained access to the Post Office Box of Mister A period.

Inside....was one letter... *(She takes letter from box with great anticipation, then opens it, to great disappointment.)* ...from me, informing him of his pretty fine. *(Then spots another letter)* And one letter, and one letter! Dated January 6th, *1906*, and here it is, Eveydence #11, written to our man by one Esther Gelfer. In Yiddish. And of all things...a love letter. An excerpt of which reads as follows— "If you must know...I am in love with you. Hopelessly. You probably don't remember me, but I remember you. In our town of misery, you suddenly appeared, and whistling that *funny little song.*" Make a note of that. *(Draws a musical note on the blackboard)* ..."I had never seen you in Zabludow before that day two years ago, the day the man with the phoneygraph came to get our voices on that machine, but I was smitten—you were shy, and knew every language under the sun, and I invited you back to my embarrassing little room. I was young, I was confused and you gallantly refused to lie with me. You refused to even sit down, in fact, and you left in a hurry, in a sweat, nervously, endearingly, and left your jacket behind. At any rate, I know you

are well-traveled, and I have emigrated to
Amerikay and this is my address and if ever
you wish to reclaim your jacket, it is here...
and I am here...I am here... Waiting..."

*(She grunts, strangely moved by the letter. Pause.
She grunts again. Then she snaps out of it, and we
see a slide with map of Zabludow and a slide of Polish
protesters)*

LIBRARIAN: She must have left Zabludow after the
Revolution of 1905, Radical Jews in Russia and
Congress Poland joining Anti-Czarists demanding
democratic elections, and Czarist authorities
instigating pogroms to divert the masses...
heads chopped off to divert the masses...
from their heads, I suppose... Well I couldn't
stop now. No time for fried rice, it was a slow
boat to Amerikay for me, to seek Esther Gelfer..out!

*(And we hear* Yiddisher Charleston *by the old
Gilt-Edged Four, or an appropriate klezmer tune
of 1920s/30s vintage )*

LIBRARIAN: Well I got to New York. A slog and a
half, but I did it, I did it. Heart pounding, I looked
up addresses, made call after call, and at last do
you know what I found? That after being in New
York for a year and a month, Esther Gelfer moved.
To Australia. Shoot me through the eyes.
    Well, feeling down, I thought about seeing a play
that night to cheer me up, a certain French musical,
but I took in a concert instead, outside, it was free
and what the heck, and then I went swing dancing,
of all things—there's a revival apparently—

*(We hear romantic swing music, and she gradually, haltingly, rediscovers her feet)*

LIBRARIAN: —and I hadn't danced like that since....well since...maarten Roosberg held me in his arms in Hoofddorp too many years ago... oh I was high as a kite that New York night, and I bored a Japanese couple senseless explaining the Dewey Decimal System while we shared a horse and buggy through Central Park at midnight, oh it was capital T Wonderful. I mean Thrilling. Both. And. In the morning I shuffled over to the YIVO Institute for Jewish Research and its Archives of Sound Recordings and Photo Archives, oh yes, we librarians know just where to go for the references, and I unearthed this little item.

*(We see a slide of a shtetl in 1904 with ethnographic surveyor with recording equipment)*

LIBRARIAN: Eveydence #13A—an ethnographic surveyor with recording equipment in Zabludow in April, 1904. And do you know who that is, that gentleman to the left with his head just out of view? *(Significantly)* Neither do I.
   But! Eveydence #13B happens to be this— *(Holds up a battered tape recorder [preferably quite out of date])* —a recording from an Edison cylinder *(Also holds up an Edison cylinder)* —one of the very ones made on that Zabludow day. Now listen. *(She plays tape, and we hear scratchy recording of person speaking Yiddish, with whistling very faintly in background)* That's Yiddish you're hearing, but listen harder. Do you hear that? In the background? That...whistling? What is that? Do you recognize it? It isn't a Polish folk song,

no, nor a Jewish one neither, no. No, it's a little
number entitled *When it's Nighttime in Italy*—
*(Sings)*
When it's Nighttime in Italy,
It's Wednesday over here,
When it's Fish Day in Germany,
You can't get shaved in Massachusetts" etcetera.
First recorded and released by Billy Jones and his
Orchestra, in *New York* in *April 1904! (Significantly)*
And now here it is, being whistled— *(Perhaps
circling drawing of man and the musical note)*
—by some unidentified personage, in a tiny
remote shtetl in Poland *the very same month*!?
Well wouldn't it be just like our well-traveled man,
as Esther writes, and I quote—to "whistle that
funny little song" in the background thus ensuring
that he would be recorded—incognito, but *in
perpetuity*—that he would *leave his mark*! Well it
was on to Australia!, find Gelfer, I *had* to. And it
was on the way, and only then, that I remembered
something...I only had a week of sick leave...
and I had been gone... *(Figures in head)* ...a month
and a half...I...was screwed. *(Disturbed)* Still. We'll...
proceed. We'll...proceed.

*(We see a slide of Australia)*

LIBRARIAN: Australia, and what did I find. Dear
Esther Gelfer. Dead. For thirty-five years. And
what did I expect? A one hundred and twenty-one
year old woman to answer all my questions? Yes.
I did find a chest of Esther's effects *(Indicating
suitcase of scraps)* there in the attic of her niece, now
living outside Brisbane. Dear...dead...Esther Gelfer,
there I stood...amongst the ephemera of your life.

*(More introspective)* There's a word. Ephemera.
From "ephemeral"—short lived—like those
insects, the ephemerids, *(Draws a mayfly on the
chalkboard)* mayflies living a day and all to find
their perfect mate, and then....die... *(She erases the
mayfly.)* ...Esther Gelfer...never-married... Why?
Not for waiting I hope. Waiting for the Wandering
Jew to settle down, oh poor esther, cupid *is* cruel.
Or blind. Ignorant. What cruelty isn't from
blindness and ignorance... Underneath the lintel...
a cobbler told a man with a cross to shove on...
and that made all the difference. *(Suddenly, she
seems overcome, voice cracking)* ...Underneath the
lintel...underneath the lintel...it's supposed to
be an innocent place...where girls kiss their
sweethearts good night...in the first bloom of
love...Maarten Roosberg...wearing those eyes of
his... *(Weeps)* he *did* love me...he said so...and what
did I do? ...And what did I do? ...I must have been
standing in an ice bucket—blazing heart...cold
feet... *(Pause)* ...and he married another, I think...
he's gone, who knows where he is now...gone,
that much I know... *(Pause)* ...but you can't live
with regrets, of course not...how was I to know he
was the one...and only... *(Full breakdown, or simply
fighting tears and losing)* no, move on..move on....
A...a...magician tells you to choose any card in
the deck, *(Increasingly bitter)* and so with free will
you do choose...but you don't realize the magician
has subtly forced you to pick the exact card he
wanted you to pick all along. Magicians call that a
"Hobson's Choice." And in life we think we make
choices...but they're Hobson's Choices. So who
is this Hobson? Who is this magician gulling us?

That's the question. Simply something named
Chance? Or Fate? *(Looking up)* Or Something Else...
*(Still fragile from breakdown)* In the hope chest of
Esther Gelfer— *(Pulls from box—)* a raggedy old
jacket, and on the jacket, a faded yellow star,
yes, like the type Jews were forced to wear in
Augsburg *in the fifteenth century*, yes, and in the
jacket—a coin. An old coin. A roman coin, from
the time of Tiberius. Issued? 37 A D. Eveydence?
#16, underlined, circled, with exclamation points
and arrows pointing to it! *(Emotionally)* That night,
outside Brisbane, I stared up at the stars until the
old orbs watered— "how very....high they are..."
...Unreachable, that's the word...and a line from
Job out of the blue blazed across the brain like
a comet— "Hitherto shalt thou come...but no
further..." But no, I'd have none of that talk. I was
in for it now, Hobson knows I hadn't a choice,
it was a world tour to track down this rapscallion,
with the Baedeker's as my guide and clue-filled
companion, for curse it all, if it's really him, then
he's out there-he lives, he lives!

*(We hear the jaunty* Freilach Yidelach *by Dave Tarras
[or a similarly spirited klezmer tune of 20s/30s vintage
by Tarras or Naftule Brandwein] as—)*

LIBRARIAN: *(Paging through Baedeker's, looking at
margins)* Let's see, he knows German, and Italian....
So I went back to Germany, then Italy, then all
over the world, where I found Graffiti written
in every language, including Welsh, and saying
especially this— *(Writes on board or wall)* "I Was
Here."

*(We see slides of Acropolis and bathroom stall.)*

LIBRARIAN: To Greece, then France, and I found the words on the side of the Acropolis, and in a bathroom stall in the Paris Metro, "I was here," "I was here"—

*(We see slides of Norwegian coast, totem pole, Mayan temple, etc.)*

LIBRARIAN: —on a rock in Norway, on a totem pole near Juneau, on the thirty-first step of a Mayan temple in Uxmal...on a park bench in Stamford, Connecticut, on a statue on Easter Island..."I was here," "I was here," "I was here," *(Perhaps writes on wall)* "I was here..."!

*(Music out. Pause. And calmly—)*

LIBRARIAN: But you might say..."Yes, but look here...those words could have been written by anyone. Perhaps you're not looking for the Wandering Jew at all, but Kilroy." And I would say to that... *(Searches for answer, and finally flipping the bird with both hands at the audience, in exasperation)* ...Fuck you! *(Then sincerely shocked at her behavior—)* And then I would apologize *profusely*, and dig about in my box of scraps for some more tangible proof.... *(Thinks, eyes light up, and pulls from box, now a little uncomfortably frantic)* ...Ah! Oh hoh! Look at this! Now look at this, look at this... Ripped from the Baedeker's...I took it from the Baedeker's... *(She holds up scrap with label dangling from it.)* —an illustration of the ruins in Rome. But by now I was learning to shift my focus, follow the blur in the periphery, look in the margins, the fringes, for that's where our man and The Truth have set up shop. So I peered very

closely at the illustration of the ruins, and there
in the corner, very small, a drawing of moths,
for flavor....

*(We see series of slides of the illustration, zooming in
until we see the moths, with words on the wing—
backwards—as if an impression from the page opposite)*

LIBRARIAN: ...but look at the wings—there's words
on them, a ghostly vestige—they must have come
from the page opposite, from years of the two
pages being pressed together—you see? Yes? Yes?
Yes? —But no! The words don't correspond, so we
can only assume that at one point a piece of paper
had been inserted *between* the pages, and there
was!, and I tracked it down!, and it's this! —a
theatrical programme!, Eveydence #77, from the
year 1777! In *Holland*, for a performance entitled
"The Wandering... *(Reads surprised and profoundly
deflated)* ...Minstrel"? *(Beat)* "Minstrel?" *No.*
This said "Jew." This said "Jew." *(Stares at paper
in disbelief)* I swear to you, it was Jew. It said
*Wandering Jew*, I *saw* it... *(Now quite lost on the stage,
she reads, softly to herself, working hard to help herself
make sense of this setback)* "Wandering Minstrel"...
*(Then—)* ...Mind you...there's a smoked herring...
called a red herring...that was used at one time to
lay trails to train hunting dogs, so the dogs could
learn to track the *aforementioned earthstopped fox.*
Well. For advanced training, the red herring was
used to *divert* the dog from the trail. All very
confusing for the dog but there's solace in this—
A herring may have been a false herring, but every
false herring still *had its purpose. (Perhaps looking at
scrap then heavenward) There's never an accidental*

*herring,* oh no, every red herring, every digression, is a step, perhaps a step sideways or backwards, but it keeps you moving nonetheless.. *(Softly, perhaps realizing for first time)* ...and there's joy...too...in that... *Yes*...yes, I was back in *Holland* to dig this one up. Strode into the Hoofddorp library, as if I hadn't been gone a day. Floris van der Donk was head of acquisitions now, "congratulations," though I almost felt sorry for her, chained to a desk all the day as she was. And after a few gawping stares from the library patrons, and some rather unkind remarks about the hum wafting off my unwashed self, I was called into the offices of my superiors and told... to shove on. *(Humbled)* It was quite a blow. "...oh...well...oh...all right then...but what about my pension," I said. "Nothing doing," they said. "But....but then how will I manage? How will I enjoy a well-earned rest in my waning days?" "You won't. We're striking your name from the files, it will be as if...you were never here at all..." And I was shown out. And there on the steps, eating my chocolate from Floris, I stared in a daze from the other side of the door. At my old haunt, my second home. Underneath the lintel I stood, grappling with a thought. Yes? Should I? No? ...Yes! And I marched back in, strode straight to my desk, stole my stamper, got out the sharpest letter opener I could find, and carved deep and irrevocably into my former desk so no one could ever be mistaken, "I WAS HERE...I WAS HERE." And then, oh boy did I run away, but fast.

Fine, *(Significance of losing job sinking in a bit)* ...fine, I lost my job... *(Now more desperate)* I lost my

job... *(And full enormity hitting her)* I lost my job...
*(Clutches stamper, spluttering)* ...but I had the
history of man in my hand, and, and, *(Desperately)*
I have this... *(And pulls from box an old horse brush
[or some other antique worthless object])* This...is...
a brush. *(Stares at thing with ever-growing
incomprehension)* Still. We'll Proceed. *(More
desperately, she pulls from box, an acorn-sized item
in small pouch with label attached—)* Ah! Look at
this...look at this...this...now look at this...this this
may *look* small and insignificant, but it is actually...
the fossilized excrement of an ancient turtle.
Oh yes. And you may ask, "what does this have
to do...with the Wandering...Jew..."

*(Long pause, as she stares at fossilized excrement.
Looks all about the stage as if quite lost. All confidence
in her scraps has now left her, and she says, softly:)*

LIBRARIAN: I don't know...I don't know...I don't
know...gone...gone, the turtle goes...but leaves
a testament more enduring than any of us can
hope for... *(To excrement/audience)* ...Do you know
how Aeschylus died, that towering playwright
of ancient Greece? It has to do with turtles.
Apparently eagles pick up turtles and carry
them aloft until they find a suitable rock to drop
them on, to crack them open. One day, an eagle
thought Aeschylus' bald head...was a rock.
Exit Aeschylus. And if you think "oh dear that's
an awfully trivial death for such a grand person,"
not to worry—fourteen people in America die
every year by vending machines falling on top
of them. Vending machines—after shaking them
for the fifty cents they just devoured....Life...fifty

cents... *(Bitterly despairing)* And it's not just the
trivial deaths, no—all death has a way of making
one's life, no matter how grand, seem silly and
small—it's as if, as if Life were Beethoven's Ninth,
but instead of culminating with a choir, a hundred-
strong, it culminates with...the squeak of a dog toy.
*(Becoming increasingly agitated, bewildered, intensely
bitter and tearful)* No, no Ode to Joy, nothing
exalting, nothing exulting, just senselessness,
senselessness, nothing miraculous, just a
nuisance—Life, Love, Your One Love...your
one love... *(Pause)* ...send him away...a mistake...
too late...carry on as if it didn't matter... It Did...
It *did*...but now it doesn't...for who can hear you,
in no time at all you're shunted off yourself and
there you go-all's forgiven, if only because...
all's forgotten.....I used to be a librarian...what
have I done...I don't know..."To prove one life,
and justify another..." with scraps...I'm sorry...
I'm sorry...I'm sorry... *(She begins putting scraps back
in the box, and packing up, when suddenly she sees the
World's Fair recording in the box. Either a shellac disc
or a cassette purporting to be a recording from the
record. She picks it up, perplexed)* ...and yet...to
say....or yell out...or carve in a wall, if but once...
"I was here..."...well, there's this—last scrap,
I promise....

*(And we see a slide of the World's Fair, and of the time
capsule exhibit)*

LIBRARIAN: At the 1939 World's Fair, in Queens,
New York, a time capsule was lowered, preserving
all sorts of artifacts in a shell of titanium, to be
unearthed a thousand years hence, a declamation

of our little existence in the twentieth century....
Was our man there, being attracted to such a
notion? *(Pointing to photograph)* Is he somewhere
in this crowd? Hard to say. But. There was a
little booth at the Fair where you could make
a record of yourself...for fifty cents. A few were
left unclaimed. This *(Holding up tape or record)*
is a recording of one of them.

*(And we hear on the tape a scratchy, and eerie,
recording of an old man [preferably recorded by actor
playing* LIBRARIAN *providing the voice of an elderly
male]. The* LIBRARIAN *echoing [with beginning of
epiphany] in a whisper "and yet..." at same time as
voice in recording—)*

LIBRARIAN: "I am here...I am here...at the World's
Fair...Is it? ...Is the world fair? ...Hardly... And
yet...I'll say this...to any who can hear...I am here...
I am here...I am here...I am here...I am here...."

*(And as the recording continues with numerous
"I am here"s, the* LIBRARIAN, *overlapping, sings
slowly and softly, her eyes lighting up as a
much-desired realization sinks in—)*

LIBRARIAN:"We're here because we're here
because we're here because we're...here..."

*(The recording fades out, and with a sort of beatific
confidence—)*

LIBRARIAN:You don't have to believe me... Say I
made it all up... "She made it all up," I don't care
anymore.... I'm tired.... Yes, I'm tired...but *I'm not
stopping my pursuit neither*...no...And Why? Because
I don't think Mister A Period has stopped, no, not
given in, No, and never will. And if one day He

Above tells our man, at last, that he may lie down...he'll sit. "Sit then", he'll stand. "Stand then", he'll *walk*.

*(God increasingly angry/exasperated)*

"Walk then," *he'll dance*. On principal. No, no repentance, no—for in the greatest act of defiance known to humankind, our man *will* find a way, this I know, mark my words, to behold this hash of a creation, to take this muck and holy mess of a life, and winnow out and revel in every bit of beauty and worth that's in it so long as he's in it, so there. And so. We Shall Proceed. Although...the trail trails off. The last promising sighting of him was over fifty years ago—testimony of a fellow doing a sort of buck dance outside the fences at Buchenwald.... "The doomed souls within were probably delirious," you'll say....and what did they see after all but a ragged Jew on the other side of the camp fence... *But, you see, our man lives incognito.* He could be there everywhere you look, but you won't see him.... If in Mexico, in a sombrero he'll be. A kimono in Kyoto, a thong in New Guinea, wooden clogs in Zander aan Zee...And I'll be following just behind him.... And after all these years, both of us...beginning to learn....to *dance*....

*(Up on the Yiddish tune* Zetz *by Annie Lubin [or some spirited klezmer tune or Yiddish song from the 20s/30s] as she exits the stage, with the Baedeker's in her hand)*

END OF PLAY

# AFTERWORD

A spot of grocery shopping, a few diapers
changed, dinner, a chat on the phone, a shower,
a shave, and an arduous mission retrieving a small
round dog toy from under the couch—that has
been my day today, and all in all, little to write
home about, certainly nothing demanding deep
consideration, nothing out of the ordinary, nothing
strange. That is, if it weren't for three
incontrovertible Facts:

1) The universe contains well over 500,000,000,000
galaxies, with each galaxy containing over
1,000,000,000,000 stars, of which, our vast,
blazing and life-bestowing sun...is one.

2) The Earth is 4,600,000,000 years old, in which
time, from the Pre-Cambrian Era to the Present—
a dizzying, terrifying number of inhabitants—
amoebas and trilobites, dust mites and
Neanderthals—have all struggled to live from
one hour to the next. (Indeed, more living
creatures are in my stomach [and yours] at
this moment than the total number of human
beings that have ever existed.)

3) I will die. I will be dead in sixty years, though
it's entirely conceivable that I'll be dead before
the week is out.

And suddenly all the props holding up my warm and secure little existence are kicked away and used for kindling. The imagination is taxed to exhaustion and left numb and agape when it even begins to fathom the implications of these Facts. They beggar the most breathless hyperbole. Three simple Facts, three confirmed and undeniable Facts—the immensity of the universe, the incomprehensibly vast history of the Earth, and our inescapable mortality—loom over all of us like three paisley mastodons. When I shine these three Facts upon any moment in my life, suddenly nothing, absolutely nothing, isn't strange, bewildering, and out of all whooping. These Facts turn every memorable or trivial or utterly forgettable moment of my existence—shopping, eating trout with spouse, lying prostrate retrieving dog toy—into the Apotheosis of the Comic and Tragic, the Inconsequential and Crucial, the Banal and Profound. These Facts loom so large, in fact, that they are rather easily ignored. Three paisley mastodons get up with us in the morning and sleep with us at night, but, for the most part, they're very quiet pachyderms, and consequently, amazingly, they blur into the unimportant background, even though one day, with trumpeting bellows, they will trample me into oblivion. Time and again I explain to myself that these Facts are interesting, profound even, but not pertinent to my daily life. NO. In truth, everything else is but shadow compared to these Facts. They are the trump cards to all the ordinary cards I hold in my hand and call "my life."

I write plays to help me keep these Three Facts in the front of my head. In other words, I write to try to keep myself engaged with the Bewildering and Infinite. But why did I write UNDERNEATH THE LINTEL in particular?

All my plays are first inspired by music, and UNDERNEATH THE LINTEL was inspired particularly by certain klezmer/yiddish music from the 1920s *(And earlier)*. The "jaunty melancholy," the "dancing-despite-it-all" quality it contained, the defiance even—a certain "finding-joy-despite-all-the-evidence-to-the-contrary" quality in the music—compelled me to try to express it as a play.

In 1976, in Laetoli, in Tanzania, some members of Mary Leakey's archaeology team were throwing chunks of dried elephant dung at each other, (as archaeologists are wont to do in their free time). When one of the paleontologists dove to the ground to avoid being pelted by dung, he noticed fossilized footprints of an animal, left in hardened volcanic ash from 3.8 million years ago. After two years of excavation, all number of animal prints were discovered, including, unexpectedly, unmistakably, the footprints of hominids—our ancient australopithecine ancestors. The fact that these prints were preserved—prints by an anonymous ancestor going about a no doubt every-day activity— testifies to me of the great Conundrum of History: What is saved, and what is lost?

There used to be a sequence in UNDERNEATH THE LINTEL, that I considered and then excised

before the New York production. After the
LIBRARIAN points out the words on the moth's
wing, and calls them a "ghostly vestige," she
mentions how "vestige" comes from the Latin
word "vestigium", meaning "footprint." The
LIBRARIAN then alludes to the footprints left by
our ancestors in Laetoli, and (unbeknownst to
the LIBRARIAN), we see a slide of those Laetoli
footprints, and then a subsequent 15-second
slideshow depicting the subsequent 4-million year
history of Humankind, full of our best and worst,
and ending with a picture of a footprint left by the
first man on the moon.

I loved the idea, and it looked really horrible when
we actually tried to execute it, and then I hated the
idea. So the sequence is out. But hopefully the idea
can still be found in the play. "Still, we'll proceed,"
the LIBRARIAN says over and again, somehow
we'll proceed, we haven't a choice, and perhaps
such a sentiment has somehow driven the
evolution of humanity itself, in tiny steps.
Oh yes, we'll often go sideways or backwards,
but continue we will, and perhaps "there is joy,
too, in that."

What, after all, do we do with the fact that
suffering has dogged humanity (and certainly
not just humanity, but the 3 billion-odd species
that have populated this planet) every step of the
way? Calculated cruelty as well as utterly random
events—10 million die in the senselessness of
W W I and a woman is struck down by a frozen
block of urine. The fact that we die is a great
fat conundrum, and it will continue to be a

conundrum for me until...well until I die. What does my little life mean when set against the huge backdrop of human history? And what's human history set against the ridiculously unimaginable backdrop of the history of the universe? (at the Rose Planetarium in New York, there's a walk representing the history of the observable universe and at the end of the walk, there's a single hair, representing the 50,000 years of human existence). And what do we do with the fact that because we only live our lives once, a single event, or a single mistake, can send our lives into a wholly unanticipated and undesired direction?

The first performance of UNDERNEATH THE LINTEL in New York was scheduled for September 18, 2001. The Soho Playhouse, being in Soho, was inaccessible for a week after the 11th, but we invited the neighborhood to see the show on the 19th. Yet although the events of 9/11 were singular and tragic, they were not, unfortunately, so out of the ordinary, when one considers the whole of history. On September 11, people were murdered out of anger and ignorance, victims who didn't want to die, and weren't expecting to die just then. Considered in this light, such events occur on larger and smaller scales every day, and have been occurring every day for thousands of years.

So it was while I was listening to the klezmer music, and trying to think of a dramatic structure that would allow me to encompass a lot of history (in lieu of the Three Facts), that I remembered the story of the Wandering Jew. Now I was quite aware that the myth of the Wandering Jew was originally an anti-semitic tale, but the myth had taken on more complex meanings in its 700-odd year history, and I felt, besides, that an artist can always appropriate myths for his own ends.

(I would later discover that a film made in Yiddish by Jews in the early 1930s called *The Wandering Jew* was made to warn a generally ignorant world of the growing Nazi menace. In the film, the Wandering Jew is depicted as a noble figure, bearing witness to history. I've received letters calling UNDERNEATH THE LINTEL anti-Semitic, and other letters calling it "anti-Christian" [for the portrayal of a cruel Christ]. I've also received letters calling the play too "pro-Zionist." So hey ho.)

In a sense, despite the Wandering Jew's seemingly unique situation, his predicament is the predicament of all humanity—he made a mistake, a single mistake "underneath the lintel", when he put fear and self-interest ahead of compassion. Every one does it all the time. And he was forced to live with that mistake the rest of his days. Did the punishment fit the crime? No. But that's often true of punishments and crimes. And even though he was condemned to live for a near-eternity, the fact that he is not allowed to be anything more than a myth (by not being allowed to communicate his existence to his fellow man) puts him in practically the same spot as the rest of humanity; namely, that his life means seemingly next-to-nothing in the great scope of history.

*However*, he is a human being, and he isn't going to give up so easily. Humanity inevitably finds the strength, despite our mistakes and tragedies, to rebuild, to persevere, to proceed, until death does us in. Graffiti throughout the ages (in a Lascaux cave or on a New York subway train) testify to the fundamental human need to affirm our own existence to each other and to the Heavens. For our LIBRARIAN, the scraps left behind by the alleged Wandering Jew prove that he will never stop seeking "a way around" God's edict. And if the Wandering Jew has been condemned by God to witness thousands of years of human suffering, then almost in defiance, he will seek out all that is good and worthy and beautiful, and if he is forced to "walk", he'll do God one better and Dance. Which of course, God no doubt wanted all along. This is the defiance, sadness, and hope I found expressed so fully in the Klezmer music I had been listening to.

The LIBRARIAN made a mistake underneath the lintel—sending the one man she ever loved away. Her ensuing, long-sublimated spiritual crisis feeds her determination to find meaning in the clues she uncovers.

But my point isn't that we should all believe in the Wandering Jew, or even in God, for that matter. Rather, anything at all—for the LIBRARIAN it was an impossibly overdue book—can be an invitation to the miraculous. And also this: That in the face of overwhelming existential bewilderment and terrible suffering, to respond with a little defiant dancing (in all its myriad forms) is a very human and very wondrous thing.

On one end of a spectrum is Coincidence, on the other end Profound Serendipity. The only difference between the two is how much meaning we choose to ascribe to a particular event. I'm still working out where on the spectrum I should put the following:

A few months back, I was paging through an Encyclopedia of Philosophy when I came across the word "Sublime", which is defined as "the presence of transcendent vastness or greatness.... While in one aspect, it is apprehended and grasped as a whole, it is felt as transcending our normal standards of measurement.... It involves a certain baffling of our faculty with feeling of limitation akin to awe and veneration; as well as a stimulation of our abilities and elevation of the self in sympathy with its object."

The word "Sublime" comes from "sub" (**Under**) + limen (which, like "limit", is a word derived originally from..."**lintel**")

Though we rarely recognize the place, underneath the lintel is where each of us stands every day, every moment, of our life.

# SLIDE LIST

Below is a list of the slides used in the
Off-Broadway production
4 slides of various London sites
1 slide of a building standing in for the Bonn
"Municipal Transportation Headquarters"
3 slides of W W I soldiers in the trenches
1 slide of a page from "Thomas Wright's Account
Book" (created for production, modified from
*Henry Will Account Book*, compiled by Donald L
Fennimore, Masthof Press (Route 1, Box 20,
Morgantown, PA 19543), © 1996)
1 slide of Joseph Wright's painting, *The Earthstopper*
4 slides "zooming in" on the image of "a man in
a funnel-shaped hat" (The image for the Off-
Broadway production came from *Jewish Art,
Grace Cohen Grossman, Hugh Lauter Levin
Associates, Inc, © 1995, The Schocken Institute for
Jewish Research, Jerusalem*, but other sources exist
for similar images)
1 slide of a Wandering Jew (*Zebrina Pendula*)
houseplant
1 slide of Beijing
1 slide of a smaller Chinese city (to stand in for
Dingtao)
1 slide of an old map of Poland with "Zabludow"
circled

1 slide depicting a gathering of anti-czarist
protesters (production image came from *Image
Before My Eyes, Lucjan Dobroszycki and Barbara
Kirshenblatt-Gimblett, Schocken Books, © 1977,
p 110)*
1 slide depicting the "ethnographic surveyor"
(production image came from *Image Before My
Eyes (see above), p 17)*
1 slide of Sydney Australia
1 slide of rural Australia (for "outside Brisbane")
1 slide of the Acropolis in Athens
1 slide of a bathroom stall
1 slide of a rock on the coast of a Norwegian town
1 slide of a totem pole in Alaska
1 slide of a Mayan temple
1 slide of a park bench
1 slide of a statue on Easter Island
1 slide of a drawing of roman ruins with a
drawing of moths almost imperceptible in
the corner
3 slides "zooming in" on the moths, to see,
imprinted backward on the brown of the wing,
the white vestige of words (This was created
for production using clip art of roman ruins
combined with the image of a moth with words
imprinted on its wing, from author's private
collection)
1 slide depicting the Trylon and Perisphere from
the New York World's Fair of 1939
1 slide depicting the time capsule exhibit from that
fair